FROM FARM TO YOU

Chocolate

Carol Jones

CHELSEA HOUSE
PUBLISHERS
A Haights Cross Communications ✦ Company
Philadelphia

This edition first published in 2003 in the United States of America by Chelsea House Publishers, a subsidiary of Haights Cross Communications.

Chelsea House Publishers
1974 Sproul Road, Suite 400
Broomall, PA 19008-0914

The Chelsea House world wide web address is www.chelseahouse.com

Library of Congress Cataloging-in-Publication Data Applied for.
ISBN 0-7910-7008-5

First published in 2002 by
MACMILLAN EDUCATION AUSTRALIA PTY LTD
627 Chapel Street, South Yarra, Australia, 3141

Copyright © Carol Jones 2002
Copyright in photographs © individual photographers as credited

Edited by Anne McKenna
Text design by Judith Summerfeldt Grace
Cover design by Judith Summerfeldt Grace

Printed in China

Acknowledgements
The author wishes to thank Peter Wilson and Fiona Kennedy of Kennedy and Wilson Chocolate for their help with the writing of this book.

Cover photographs: Chocolate freckles courtesy of Imageaddict, liquid chocolate courtesy of Artville.

APL/Corbis © Bettmann, p. 6, © Owen Franken, pp. 18 (top), 20, 28 (Spain), © Wolfgang Kaehler, p. 19 (bottom right), © Adam Woolfitt, p. 28 (Austria), p. 28 © Christian Sarramon, © Jacqui Hurst, p. 28 (Belgium); Artville, pp. 8–9, 28 (France); Cadbury Chocolate, p. 24; Coo-ee Historical Picture Library, p. 7 (top and bottom); Copper Leife/Craig Forsythe, pp. 25–6, 28 (Italy and England), p. 29 (Australia); Getty Images/Photodisc, pp. 28 (Netherlands), 28–9 (map), Tony Stone, p. 4; Imageaddict, p. 9 (bottom); Carol Jones, pp. 3 (top right and bottom left), 10–11 (main), 10 (bottom right), 11 (bottom), 12–15; Lindt Chocolates, pp. 3 (top left and bottom right), 16–17, 18 (bottom), 19 (top and bottom left), 21 (top and bottom), 22–3, 28 (Switzerland); Photolibrary.com, pp. 5, FoodPix, p. 10 (bottom left).

While every care has been taken to trace and acknowledge copyright, the publisher tenders their apologies for any accidental infringement where copyright has proved untraceable.

Contents

The world of chocolate

The smooth, creamy treat we know as chocolate is made from the bitter beans of the cacao tree.

The beans are the seeds of a fruit called a pod. They are roasted and ground to a powder. These ground beans give us cocoa, which is used to make chocolate.

Some chocolate lovers prefer their chocolate bitter. Others like the creamy taste of milk chocolate with plenty of sugar in it.

Sweet or bitter, dark or milk, there is a chocolate to suit almost every taste. It can have nuts or fruits added to it. It can be molded to any shape, or filled with **liqueur**. Foods can be flavored with it or dipped into it. It can be made into a hot, sweet drink or used as a sauce.

Whatever form it takes, chocolate is a favorite treat around the world.

Almost everyone loves to eat chocolate.

The history of chocolate

No one knows exactly when chocolate was first used as a food, but people were writing about it 1,500 years ago.

It is believed that cacao trees are native to South America but were taken north to Central America. The ancient Mayan people lived on the narrow land between modern-day Mexico and Guatemala in Central America. To the Maya, the cacao tree was the 'Tree of the Gods'. They drank frothy chocolate drinks whipped with vanilla and other spices at religious festivals.

The Mayan people mysteriously disappeared more than 1,000 years ago. The Aztec people who took over their land also loved the flavor of chocolate, which they called *cacahuatl*. They made offerings of jugs of chocolate to their gods.

The people of Central America still grow and **harvest** the cacao tree. These workers are shown with piles of harvested cacao pods.

Strange but true!

The Aztecs kept their cacao beans in treasure houses and used them as money. A tomato cost one bean, an egg cost three beans, a mule was 50 beans and a human slave cost 100 beans.

When Spanish explorers arrived in Central America in the early 1500s, they took the cacao bean back to Spain. At first, the Spanish drank their chocolate hot and spicy like the Aztecs, but they soon learned that they liked it better when sugar was added to it.

In the 1600s, drinking chocolate became popular throughout Europe. But Spain controlled trade with Central America, where the cacao trees were grown, and the Spanish kept the recipe for drinking chocolate a secret. Chocolate was very expensive because the beans had to be transported so far. Governments also put heavy taxes on it, so chocolate became a drink that only rich people could afford.

The Spanish explorer, Cortés (with sword) meeting the Aztec emperor, Montezuma (wearing head-dress)

Firsts

The first European to take chocolate back to Europe was probably Don Hernándo Cortés, explorer and leader of the Spanish army in Mexico in the 1500s. The Aztec emperor, Montezuma served chocolate in golden goblets to Cortés and his army.

At first, chocolate was taken only as a drink. In England, chocolate houses became popular. Rich people went there to drink chocolate and gossip with their friends.

In 1828, Dutch chocolate maker van Houten invented a way to squeeze out the **cocoa butter** (oil) from the beans to make cocoa powder. In 1847, J. S. Fry and Sons of England discovered how to combine the cocoa powder with sugar and cocoa butter to make bars of dark bitter chocolate. Then in 1876, Daniel Peter of Switzerland found a way of adding milk to chocolate.

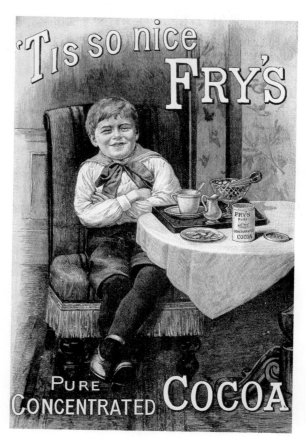

An 1893 advertisement for Fry's cocoa powder

A 1910 advertisement for chocolates

Famous chocolate

In 1900, an American called Milton Hershey introduced the chocolate Hershey Bar. During World War II, Hershey Bars became famous because the chocolate bars were part of the food rations for American soldiers. The soldiers shared them with hungry people. Today, United States Army rations still include chocolate bars.

Kinds of chocolate

Chocolate comes in many shapes and forms but there are four main kinds.

1. Cocoa powder

After some of the cocoa butter has been removed from the roasted and ground beans, the remaining cocoa is ground to a fine powder. Cocoa powder can be used for drinking and cooking. Drinking chocolate has sugar added to the cocoa.

2. Milk chocolate

Milk chocolate is a mixture of sugar, **cocoa liquor** (which becomes a solid **cocoa mass** when cool), cocoa butter and milk. Fresh milk does not mix well with cocoa liquor, so dried milk powders or **condensed milk** are used instead.

Milk chocolate makes popular bunnies at Easter time.

3. Dark chocolate

Dark or plain chocolate does not have added milk. It contains cocoa butter, cocoa liquor and usually some sugar. It can be bittersweet, semisweet or sweet. Bittersweet chocolate is often used for baking.

4. White chocolate

White chocolate is white because it has no cocoa liquor, just the pale cocoa butter and sugar.

A selection of filled dark and milk chocolates

Other uses for cocoa butter

Cocoa butter will keep for a long time without refrigeration. It also absorbs scents well. Because of this it is sometimes used for making face creams, make-up removers and ointments.

How chocolate is made

Although most chocolate is made in large **automated** factories, there are many small specialist chocolate makers. Some make plain or milk chocolate bars. Others specialize in filled chocolates.

The chocolate maker shown here is making milk chocolate in small molded shapes. She makes small amounts of expensive chocolates, which are sold in chocolate shops, gift shops and restaurants.

Vanilla pods and flower

The melting tank

Ingredients

To make these milk chocolate shapes, the chocolate maker uses the following ingredients:

- cocoa mass (or liquor) — made from roasted cacao beans ground to a paste
- extra cocoa butter — oil pressed from cocoa mass
- skim milk powder
- sugar
- vanilla beans — a spice
- lecithin — an **emulsifier**.

Tools and equipment

Some of the tools of this chocolate maker are:

- scales — for weighing the ingredients
- conch — for heating and **kneading** the chocolate
- melting tank — for melting the ingredients
- tempering machine — for heating and cooling the chocolate
- molding machine — for the molding process
- molds — for molding the chocolate mixture into shapes
- cooling tunnel — for cooling and setting the chocolate
- trays and shelves — for stacking the chocolates ready for packing.

The tempering machine

Method

Weighing the ingredients

The chocolate maker uses cocoa liquor from many different countries such as Papua New Guinea, Venezuela, Indonesia, Malaysia and Colombia. The cocoa liquor and all ingredients are weighed. Then everything but the lecithin is put into the conch, according to the chocolate maker's recipe.

The milk chocolate being made contains 48 percent cocoa liquor. Dark chocolate contains 70 percent cocoa liquor. Bittersweet chocolate has 81 percent cocoa liquor. It is tasty, but very bitter!

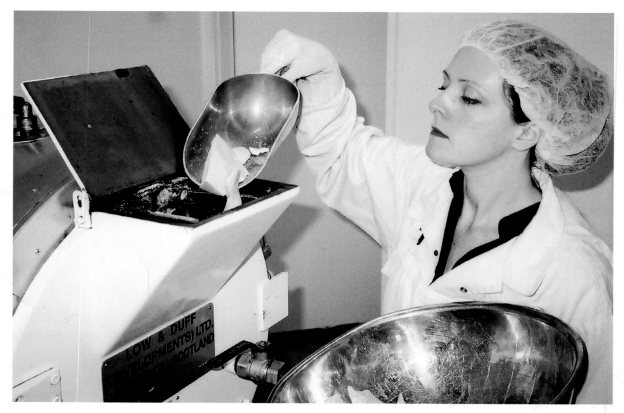

Putting the cocoa butter in the conch

Conching the ingredients

The first conch machines looked like conch shells, which is how they got their name. The conch heats the ingredients and its heavy rollers knead them backwards and forwards for three days. The ingredients are conched until the chocolate mixture is completely smooth.

Just before the conching is finished, a small amount of lecithin is added to help make the chocolate smooth. When the conching is finished, the chocolate maker releases a tap so that the liquid chocolate runs into a melting tank. Later, the conching machine is rinsed out with cocoa butter so that it is clean for the next batch of ingredients.

After three days in the conching machine, chocolate is smooth and pours easily from the tap.

The chocolate maker scrapes the last of the chocolate from the conching machine.

Tempering the mixture

The chocolate mixture stays in the melting tank for about one hour. This tank holds the chocolate at a temperature of 113 degrees Fahrenheit (45 degrees Celsius). The chocolate maker then pours the mixture into the tempering machine where it is tempered for 15 minutes.

The tempering machine cools the chocolate and then heats it again. This removes any unwanted crystals by evening out the fat particles. If the chocolate is not tempered it turns crumbly, rather than fine and shiny with a good snap.

The tempering machine has many colored dials and buttons which help control the temperature of the chocolate.

Molding the chocolate

The chocolate maker places several molds on the molding machine. This machine vibrates very quickly so that the chocolate in the molds is evened out and no air is trapped underneath. The chocolate maker pours liquid chocolate into the molds as they vibrate on the molding machine. Any extra chocolate is scraped from the top of the molds.

The chocolate maker works fast to fill each chocolate mold before the chocolate starts to harden.

Cooling the chocolate

The mold is placed into a long cooling tunnel. It moves through the tunnel on a **conveyor belt** where it cools and sets. This takes 15 to 30 minutes, depending on the type of chocolate and mold. At the end of the cooling tunnel the mold lands on a waiting tray. The chocolate maker taps the mold gently to release the chocolates. Then she stacks the trays on shelves ready to be packed the next day.

Putting the molds into the cooling tunnel

The cooling tunnel runs the length of the room in the small chocolate factory.

Packing the chocolates

The chocolates are packed by hand. They are wrapped carefully in paper and placed in small boxes ready for delivery to stores and restaurants.

Packing the chocolates into boxes

The chocolate factory

Most chocolates are made in large factories. Thousands of chocolates are produced every hour in these fully automated factories.

From farm to consumer

Follow the flowchart to see how cacao beans are farmed, **processed**, made into chocolate in large factories and then transported to stores for sale to the **consumer**.

Read more about each stage of the chocolate-making process and how chocolate is marketed and sold on pages 18 to 27. Look for the flowchart symbols that represent each stage of the process.

Farming cacao trees
Cacao beans come from trees grown on large **plantations** in tropical countries. When ripe, the beans are harvested.

Packaging the chocolate
Packaging materials may be manufactured elsewhere and delivered to the factory. Chocolate is packaged for stores or other large consumers.

Transport and storage
The packaged chocolate is stored in air-conditioned warehouses until it is transported to stores.

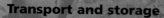

Transport and storage

After harvesting, beans are dried and transported to the nearest port for shipment.
When the beans reach their destination, they are then stored in large towers called silos ready for processing.

Processing the beans

At the processing factory, the beans are cleaned, roasted, cracked and crushed.

Manufacturing the chocolate

At the chocolate factory the processed beans are blended with sugar and milk to make milk chocolate that is ready for packaging.

Transport and storage

The processed beans are transported to the chocolate factory.

Marketing and selling chocolate

Chocolate can be sold locally or exported to other countries.

Buying chocolate

The consumer can buy chocolate from many different stores. It will keep for six to 12 months in a cool, dry place.

Farming cacao trees

Cacao trees are grown in tropical countries. Some cacao trees are grown on large company plantations. Others are grown on small family farms.

Cacao trees need heavy rainfall and warm temperatures all year round. Young trees must be watered during dry times. Trees are sprayed to protect them from pests and diseases. They also need protection from wind and hot sun. Seedlings are usually planted in the shade of another useful tree, such as a banana or rubber tree.

Cacao trees grow from seeds or cuttings. In their fourth or fifth year they bear fruit. The melon-shaped fruits, called pods, grow on the trunk and main branches. The pods ripen to gold, orange or red. Each pod contains 20 to 50 seeds, which are called cacao beans.

The cacao pod on the tree

Inside a ripe cacao pod

Transport and storage

Dried beans are packed into sacks. Villagers sometimes carry the sacks on their heads, or move them by mule or canoe to the nearest road or railroad.

Collecting and drying the beans

There are usually two harvests a year. Pickers use long-handled steel knives to reach the highest pods and **machetes** to reach the lower ones. Gatherers follow the pickers and collect the pods in baskets. A pod breaker uses a machete to split open up to 500 woody shells in an hour. Then the beans are scooped from the pods. It takes nearly 1,000 cacao beans to make about two pounds (one kilogram) of chocolate.

Harvesting the ripe pods

Heaps of beans are covered with leaves. They begin to **ferment** and change color. Then they are laid on bamboo mats to dry in the sun.

The beans in these sacks will be loaded onto ships and transported to Switzerland.

The beans are dried in the sun.

The sacks are loaded onto ships to be transported to cooler countries for processing.

Plantation workers

Farmers

Harvest workers

At the processing factory, beans are cleaned, roasted, cracked and crushed to make cocoa liquor.

Before the beans can be roasted, they are passed through a cleaning machine to remove unwanted **pulp**, bits of pod, stones and leaves. Then they are graded and weighed.

Cacao beans being graded

The beans are roasted in large rotating drums for up to two hours. The time depends on whether the beans are to be used for cocoa or chocolate. As the beans turn in the drum, moisture is removed and the beans turn dark brown.

Processing workers
Food scientists
Food technologists
Engineers
Production-line workers
Transport workers

Transport and storage

Before they are processed, beans are stored in large silos. Storage areas are kept away from other buildings so that the cacao beans do not absorb strong smells.

Cracking and crushing the beans

After roasting, a machine called a cracker and fanner cracks the shells. Mechanical sieves separate large and small pieces of shell. A fan of air blows the shell away from the meat, which is called the 'nib'. Nibs are crushed between large grinding stones or heavy steel discs. The friction heats the cocoa butter in the beans to a liquid, which cools to form solid blocks of cocoa mass or liquor.

To make cocoa powder for drinking and cooking, the cocoa butter is squeezed from the cocoa mass by giant **hydraulic** presses and then refined before being packaged as cocoa. The remaining cocoa butter is used to make chocolate.

Huge presses squeeze cocoa mass to make the cocoa butter used in chocolate making.

Cocoa cakes leaving the hydraulic press. These cakes are crushed to make cocoa powder.

Conservation

The waste products from processing cocoa are very useful. The unwanted shells are pressed into shapes and sold as animal food. They can also be used as fuel or **fertilizer**.

Some processing plants are located at chocolate factories. Others are located farther away, so the cocoa products need to be transported to the chocolate factories.

Manufacturing the chocolate

Large chocolate factories are usually fully automated. The chocolate automatically travels from machine to machine. Workers operate the machines and check the chocolate at each stage. Each factory is different but the process is similar.

To make milk chocolate, cocoa mass, sugar and milk are blended in a large heated vat for several hours to remove the water. The paste is then ground between heavy rollers until the mixture forms a powder called 'crumb'. Cocoa butter is added and the crumb travels through steel rollers. It is churned or conched backwards and forwards for up to 72 hours, depending on the quality of the chocolate. Other factories use a machine that works like a giant egg-beater.

Heavy steel rollers grind the paste to a crumb.

Chocolate is churned in the conching machine.

Transport and storage

Ingredients are stored in large tanks and silos. The Hershey factory can store enough beans to make 5 billion chocolate bars.

Molding the chocolate

From the conch, chocolate travels to a tempering machine. It is heated and cooled to even out the fat particles in the chocolate. It is then stored in heated vats where it is stirred continuously until it is needed.

The chocolate flows through pipes to the molding machine. As the molds travel along a conveyor belt, a large hopper (like a big bin) pours the correct amount of chocolate into each mold. Other ingredients such as fruits and nuts can be added at this stage. The molds glide along the conveyor belt where they are shaken to remove air bubbles. Then they move through a cooling tunnel to set the chocolate. At the end of the tunnel the molds are tipped upside down by another machine. The chocolate falls out of the molds and remains on the conveyor belt.

The molding machine

A nut filling has been placed into this chocolate bar, which will be covered with a layer of chocolate.

Additives

Chocolate may have **additives** such as emulsifiers to make the chocolate easier to blend. Poorer quality chocolate is made with vegetable oil instead of cocoa butter.

Chocolate factory workers
Food scientists
Food technologists
Engineers
Industrial technologists
Production-line workers
Transport workers

Chocolate melts at 77 degrees Fahrenheit (25 degrees Celsius), so finished chocolate is stored in air-conditioned warehouses.

Shaped chocolate may be packaged and transported to stores or shipping ports, or sent directly to large companies.

Some chocolate is transported straight to other food **manufacturers** for making cakes, cookies, ice creams and other foods. Bulk chocolate is often transported in liquid form.

Chocolate has to be packaged before it can be shipped. Some chocolate bars are sealed in foil to keep out moisture and protect them from heat. An outer wrapper is added and the chocolate bars are packed into cartons. Other chocolate bars are wrapped in plastic packaging and sealed. Packaging is done by large, fully automated machines operating at high speed.

A company's brand name will be featured on the packaging as well as information about the ingredients in the chocolate.

Fully automated machines can wrap thousands of chocolate bars an hour.

Transport and storage

After packaging, chocolate is transported in refrigerated trucks to local stores, or it is sent to ports to be shipped overseas.

Manufacturers produce a range of chocolates as well as chocolate bars. Some machines can make hundreds of chocolates every minute by squirting out jets of chocolate into different shapes. Other machines, called enrobers, pour liquid chocolate over candy or fruit centers. Each kind of chocolate needs the right kind of packaging. Some are wrapped in foil. Others are wrapped in plastic or paper. Some are also packed in boxes and sealed in thin plastic.

The chocolate is packed into boxes ready for transporting.

Different kinds of packaging

Packaging plant workers

Engineers

Production-line workers

Graphic designers

Transport workers

Forklift drivers

Marketing and selling chocolate

Chocolate may be sold locally or exported to other countries. Chocolate companies use advertising to encourage consumers to buy their product.

Workers from the chocolate companies, called merchandisers, visit stores to make sure that the stores are receiving the kinds and amounts of chocolate the consumers want. They also organize special displays and tastings to help advertise their company's products.

Chocolate companies place advertisements in magazines or on television. They run contests on chocolate wrappers to encourage consumers to buy more of their products. Some companies have their own websites to tell consumers about their products.

Large chocolate companies research new products. They test new products by asking testers to say what they like or do not like about the product. This is called market research. It helps companies find out which products will sell well.

Stocking the chocolate aisle at the supermarket

Buying chocolate

Consumers can buy chocolates in different ways and in different sizes. They can buy chocolate in small, medium or large blocks. They can also buy mini chocolate bars in plastic bags.

Consumers can choose from many kinds of chocolate treats — chocolate bars, chocolate cakes and cookies, or a warm cup of cocoa on a cold day.

Different chocolate treats

Marketing and sales workers

Merchandisers
Shelf-fillers
Checkout operators
Managers
Graphic designers
Copywriters

Home storage

Chocolate is best stored in a refrigerator if you live in a very hot climate. Otherwise, chocolate can be stored in a cool, dry cupboard. Chocolate is best wrapped in foil and kept away from strong smells and bugs. Dark chocolate can keep for a year and milk chocolate can keep for six months.

If chocolate melts and sets again it may change color. The white flecks on the chocolate are called 'bloom'. This bloom is not harmful, but it does not look very good.

Chocolate around the world

Some of the world's oldest chocolate companies such as Cadbury, Terry's, Fry and Rowntree began in England.

Belgium exports its cooking chocolate around the world.

In the Netherlands, people sometimes sprinkle grated chocolate on their breakfast cereal.

Spanish people enjoy doughnuts with a hot chocolate dip.

A popular breakfast in France is a bowl of hot drinking chocolate and a croissant filled with chocolate.

In Italy, the town of Perugia is famous for filled chocolates such as Baci.

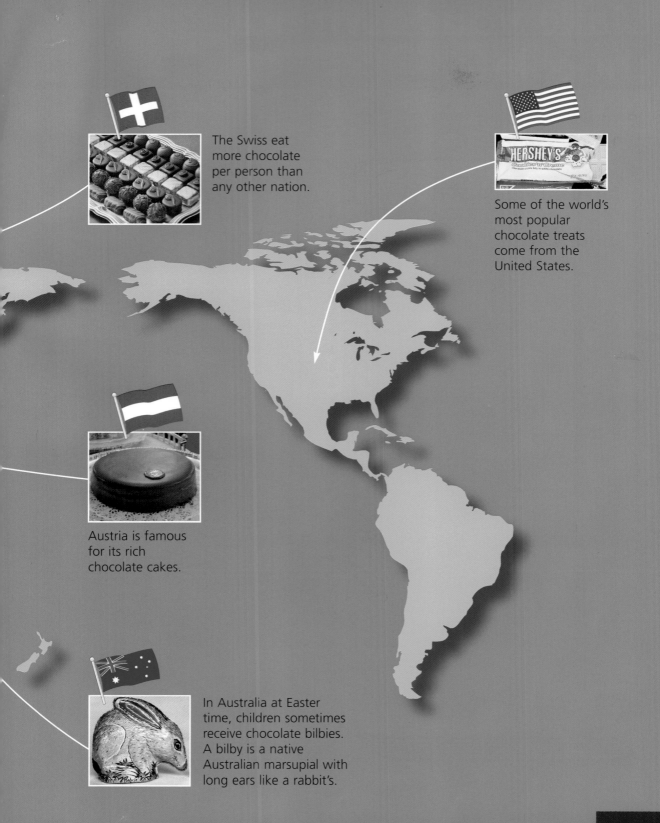

The Swiss eat more chocolate per person than any other nation.

Some of the world's most popular chocolate treats come from the United States.

Austria is famous for its rich chocolate cakes.

In Australia at Easter time, children sometimes receive chocolate bilbies. A bilby is a native Australian marsupial with long ears like a rabbit's.

Make your own hot chocolate

Use this recipe to make two mugs of hot chocolate at home with help from an adult.

Hot chocolate

Ingredients

- 4 ounces of plain dark chocolate
- 2 cups of skim or low-fat milk
- 3 drops of vanilla
- pinch of cinnamon
- pinch of ground cloves
- a little sugar to taste (if necessary)

Equipment

- medium-sized saucepan
- wooden spoon
- whisk
- two mugs

Method

1. Break the chocolate into small pieces. Place the chocolate and other ingredients into the saucepan.
2. Heat gently, stirring all the time. Do not allow the mixture to boil.
3. When the mixture is hot, take the saucepan off the heat.
4. Whisk the mixture in the saucepan until it becomes frothy.
5. Pour the mixture into mugs.

Glossary

additives   substances added to improve something

automated   machines that work with little human help

cocoa butter   a vegetable oil from the cacao tree

cocoa liquor or mass   dried, roasted and ground cacao seeds

condensed milk   thick milk with some of the water removed

consumer   person who buys goods or services

conveyor belt   an endless strip of material, such as rubber, on rollers used to move something

emulsifier   a salt that helps one substance blend with another

ferment   to cause a chemical reaction that changes the nature of food

fertilizer   a substance added to soil to help plants grow

food technologists   workers who scientifically test or treat food

harvest   pick the ripe crop

hydraulic   operated by the pressure of oil or water through a pipe

industrial technologists   workers who repair and maintain factory machines

kneading   working and pressing the chocolate mixture

liqueur   very sweet alcoholic drink

machetes   large knives

manufacturers   people or companies that make goods

plantations   farms in tropical countries that grow crops

processed   treated or prepared in a special way

pulp   soft, fleshy plant material

Index

A
additives/emulsifiers 23
advertising 26
Australia 29
Austria 28
Aztec people 5–6

B
Belgium 28

C
cacao beans 4–8, 11, 16–22
cacao pods 4, 18–19, 20
cacao seeds *see* cacao pods
cacao tree 4–6, 16, 18
Central America 5–6
cleaning 20
cocoa beans *see* cacao beans
cocoa butter 7, 8, 9, 10, 13, 21, 22
cocoa liquor 8–9, 11–12, 20–22
cocoa mass *see* cocoa liquor
cocoa powder 7–8, 21
conching 11–13, 22–23
conservation 21
consumers 16–17, 24, 26–27
cooling 11, 15, 23

D
drying 19

E
England 7, 28
Europe 6

F
farming 16, 18–19
France 28

H
harvest 16–17, 19

I
Italy 28

M
machines 11–13, 20–25
manufacturing 16–17, 22–24
marketing 17, 26
Mayan people 5
Mexico 5–6
molding 11, 14, 23

N
Netherlands 28

P
packaging 11, 15–17, 24–25
pests and diseases 19
preservation 9
processing 16–17, 20–21

R
roasting 4, 17, 20–21

S
selling 10, 16–17, 26
South America 5
Spain 6, 28
storage 16–24, 27
supermarkets 27
Switzerland 29

T
tempering 14, 23
transport 16–24

U
United States 7, 9, 22